Joseph Mazzinghi

Tiro Musicus

Being a complete introduction to the piano forte. Op. 24

Joseph Mazzinghi

Tiro Musicus
Being a complete introduction to the piano forte. Op. 24

ISBN/EAN: 9783744795982

Printed in Europe, USA, Canada, Australia, Japan

Cover: Foto ©Thomas Meinert / pixelio.de

More available books at **www.hansebooks.com**

TIRO MUSICUS,

Being a

Complete Introduction

TO THE

Piano Forte

WITH

Eight Progressive Lessons

Composed

and Fingered throughout

By

JOSEPH MAZZINGHI.

Op. 24.   Book 1st Pr. 5s.

LONDON

Printed by G. Goulding No. 6 James Street Covent Garden

N.B. These Lessons to be continued.

The first thing to be learnt is the names of the Notes on the **PIANO FORTE** in order to attain which please to observe that the white Keys are arranged equally from one end of the Instrument to the other, whereas the black Keys are placed more irregular being divided into clusters of two and three alternately, the Keys are named after the first seven Letters of the Alphabet viz: **A.B.C.D.E.F.G.**

The White Key immediately below (that is to say to the left of) the two black Keys is called **C.** in every part of the Instrument, where the two black Keys appear, and by that Note you may find all the rest, for Example, having got **C**, the next white Key above it (or to the right) is **D.** the next **E.F.G.A.B.** till you come to **C** again, which will be found in the same situation as your first **C.** that is to say below the two black Keys, you must likewise learn them backwards beginning with **C**, and proceeding to the left or downwards **B.A.G.F.E.D.** please to observe that all white Keys in the whole instrument are but a repitition of these seven Notes, they must be learnt not only backwards and forwards with great fluency, but likewise by Skips, and contrary to the natural progression as from C to E, from E to A. &c. reckoning from Note to Note as occasion may require.

Having gain'd a competent knowledge of the white Keys, we next proceed to the black Keys or Flats and Sharps. The black Key next above or to the right of C is C Sharp, that above D is D Sharp, E has no Sharp, the next above F is F Sharp, above G, G Sharp, above A, A Sharp, B has no Sharp, the black Key to the left or below D, is D Flat, below E, is E Flat, F has no Flat, below G, G Flat, below A, A Flat, B, B Flat, C has no Flat.

Hence it appears that the same Keys are made use of both for Flats and Sharps, in the different situations, those above the natural Notes being Sharps, those below them Flats.

Having fully exercised yourself in the Names of all the Keys on the Instrument, we next proceed to learn the Notes on the Paper those that have this mark 𝄞 or Cliff at the beginning are called the Treble, and are to be play'd with the right hand.

Example.

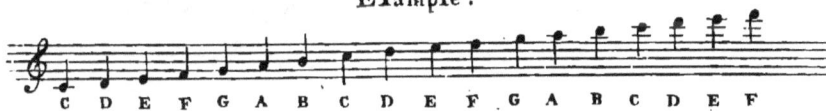

C D E F G A B C D E F G A B C D E F

Those Notes with this Mark 𝄢 at the beginning are to be play'd with the left, that being the Mark of the Bass Cliff.

F G A B C D E F G A B C D E F G A B C.

These Notes must all be learnt by heart that when they are met with in any piece of Music they may readily be known again and their Names ascertain'd.

Observe that the lowest Note in the first Example is to be found exactly in the middle of the Instrument, is therefore called middle C, being the highest Note in the Bass, and the lowest in the Treble, and by reckoning from this Note you may easily find the situation of all the rest.

For the convenience of those whose memories are weak and cannot easily acquire the Notes I have fubjoin'd the following Table, to be learnt by Heart by the Scholar feperating the lines from the Spaces that they cannot be well miftaken.

Treble Notes

Bafs Notes

The Bafs fometimes extends itself upwards into the Treble and the Treble downwards into the Bafs in which case they may be said to borrow from each other, in the following Ex=ample the Notes of both are fynonymous.

The Treble
defcending
into the Bafs

The Bafs
afcending
into the Treble

It is on this account that another Cliff called the Tenor Cliff is occasionally used in order to keep within the compafs of the five Lines; it is mark'd thus or thus & is placd fometimes on the first Line fometimes the third or fourth and where ever it ftands that Note is called C.

Before we proceed further in the Theory it will be necefsary to exercife the Scholar in the practi= cal knowledge of what has been faid already, for which purpose without looking further He may pick out the Notes both Treble and Bafs of two or three Airs that are moft familiar which will relieve the mind and awaken attention to the more obstruse parts of the Science.

NB: This Mark O fignifies the Thumb, 1 the 1ft Finger, 2 the Second, &c. &c.

OF FLATS and Sharps &c.

A Sharp is mark'd thus ♯ and if placed at the beginning of a Piece denotes that all the Notes on that Line or Space (with their Corresponding Octaves) are to be half a Tone higher thro' the whole Piece, If placd in the middle of a Tune it is confin'd to that Bar only in which it ftands.

A Flat ♭ fignifies that the Note on that Line or Space fhould be half a Tone lower fubject to the reftrictions as the foregoing.

A Natural ♮ is merely meant to restore those Notes that were before Sharp or Flat to their Natural State.

A fingle Bar | ferves to divide the measure and a double Bar || is the conclusion of each part.

A Repeat is mark'd thus 𝄇 or thus 𝄌 and means that such part of the Tune must go over again, sometimes it is join'd to the double Bar :|| which means the same thing . A Slur thus ⌢ signifies that the Notes over which it is placed shou'd be join'd together as much as possible which can only be done by keeping the finger on the Key till the next is ready . If put over two Notes of the same line or space it ought to be held out the full time of both Notes, without being struck again .

Staccato Notes thus ♩♩ or thus ♩♩ are oppos'd to the foregoing being exceeding short and pointed but care must be taken after striking the Note to stay out the full time as in these kind of Passages the Ear is apt to be deceiv'd and hurry on . A Pause ⌢ over a Note generally means a full Stop, there are different kinds of Pauses (tho' by an unaccountable defect) but one way of marking them sometimes it is meant to be short and sudden, sometimes softly sustain'd and to die away upon the Ear, at other times a gentle Cantabile or extempore flourish is proper, but these distinctions cannot be acquired but by long practice and experience .

A Shake *tr* is perform'd thus [music notation] be carefull to play the Notes equally and never finish a Shake without making a return from the Note below as no Shake can be complete without it . A Turn ∾ is used when a Note is of so short duration as not to al=

=low time for a regular Shake thus [music notation] be cautious to begin and end on the Note on which the Shake or turn is mark'd .

An inverted Turn ∾ or S is played thus [music notation] by beginning on the Note below .

There are two sorts of Measure or Time viz, Common Time and Triple Time, Common Time con= =sists of an equal number of Notes in a Bar, such as 2 Minims, 4 Crotchets, 8 Quavers &c. the usual Marks are thus 𝄴 consisting of 1 Semibreve &c. in a Bar, which is slow, thus 𝄵 somewhat quicker $\frac{2}{4}$ or 2 Crotchets in a Bar, which is quick or slow, according to the Italian Terms commonly inserted at the beginning of a Piece, for an explanation of which see the Dictionary at the end of this Book . Triple Time consists of 3. 6. 12. &c. Notes in a Bar and is mark'd thus $\frac{3}{2}$ or three Minims in a Bar $\frac{3}{4}$ or 3 Crotchets somewhat faster, this is like= =wise called Minuet time, $\frac{3}{8}$ or three Quavers very quick, but all depend on the Characters mark'd at the beginning . There are two other sorts of Measure which being a mixture of both Times are called Compound Common Time, and Compound Triple Time . Compound Common Time is mark'd thus $\frac{12}{4}$ or Twelve Crotchets in a Bar, $\frac{12}{8}$ or twelve Quavers $\frac{6}{4}$ or Six Crotchets, $\frac{6}{8}$ or Six Quavers, Compound Triple Time has these Characters, $\frac{9}{4}$ or Nine Crotchets in a Bar, $\frac{9}{8}$ or Nine Quavers, The Numbers and Proportions of all different Times may be found by inspecting the following Example .

Example

Common Time   Triple Time

[music notation]

Compound Common Time

[music notation]

Compound Triple Time

[music notation]

An Apogiatura or diminutive Note placed before a large one thus or fufpends or borrows half of it, So that a Minim with a fmall Crotchet before.it is play'd like two Crotchets play'd thus and fo in the fame proportion of all the other Notes. When an Apogiatura comes before a dotted Note it takes away two thirds of the Note Ex: play'd thus

The Notes, their Names Proportions, Refts &c.

A Speck (or Dot) after any Note or Rest makes it half as long again.

INTRODUCTION.

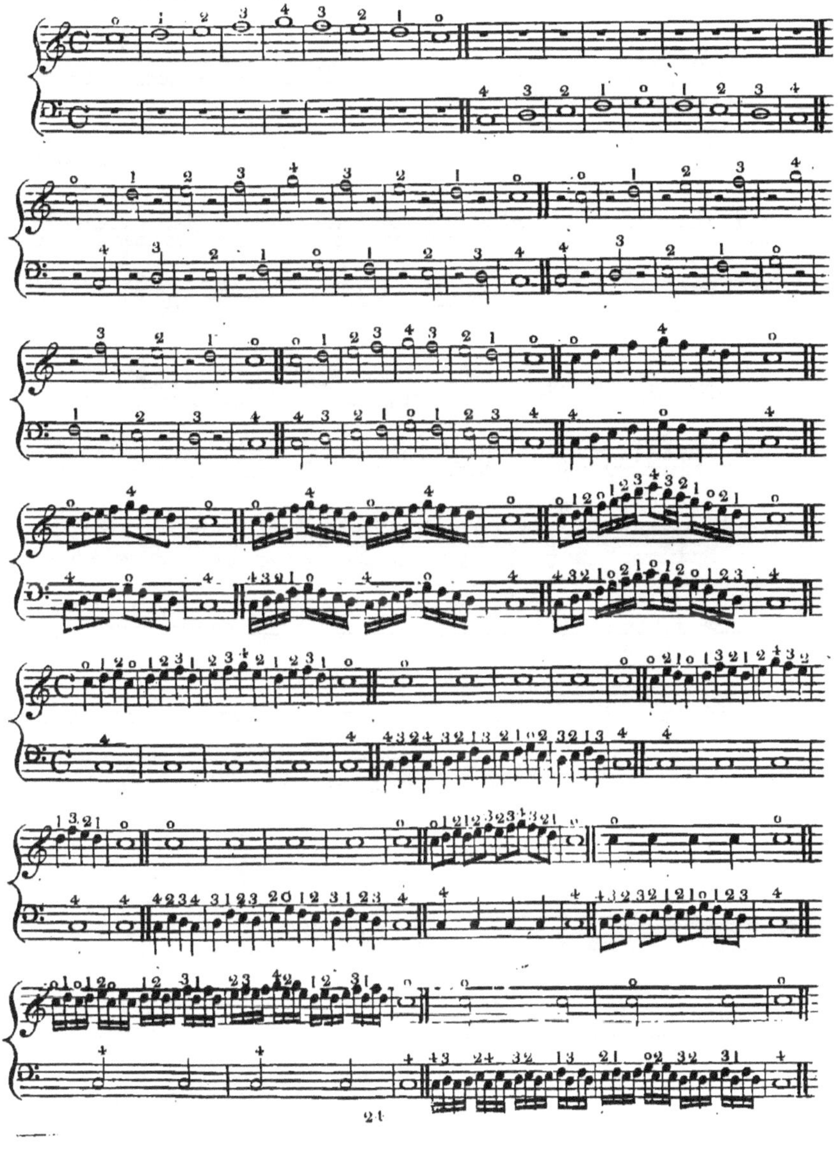

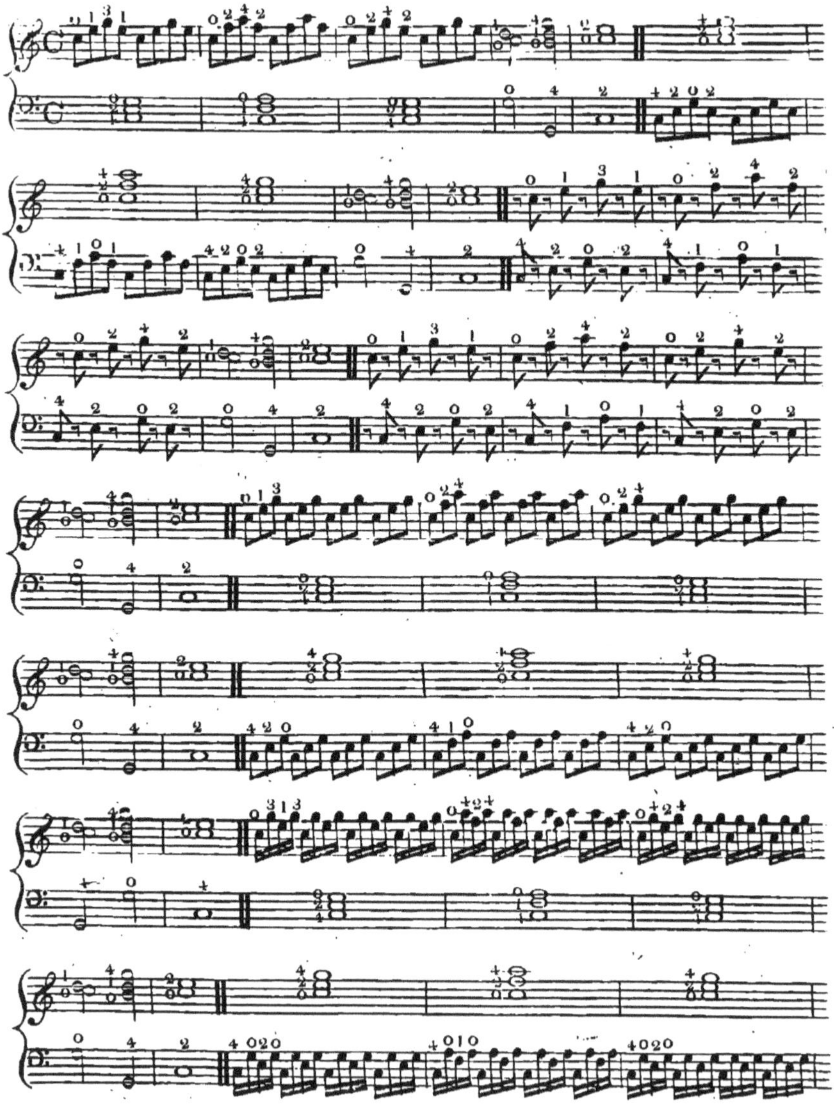

24

LESSON. I.

Andante.

Allegretto

Andantino

Lesson.II.
Allegretto

24

Larghetto

Allegretto

LESSON.III
Andante

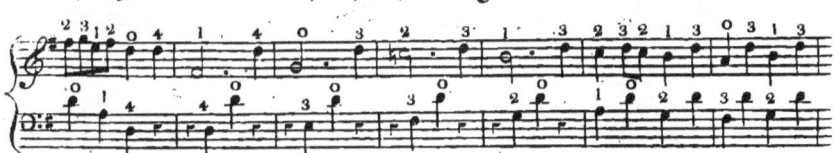

24

Grazioso

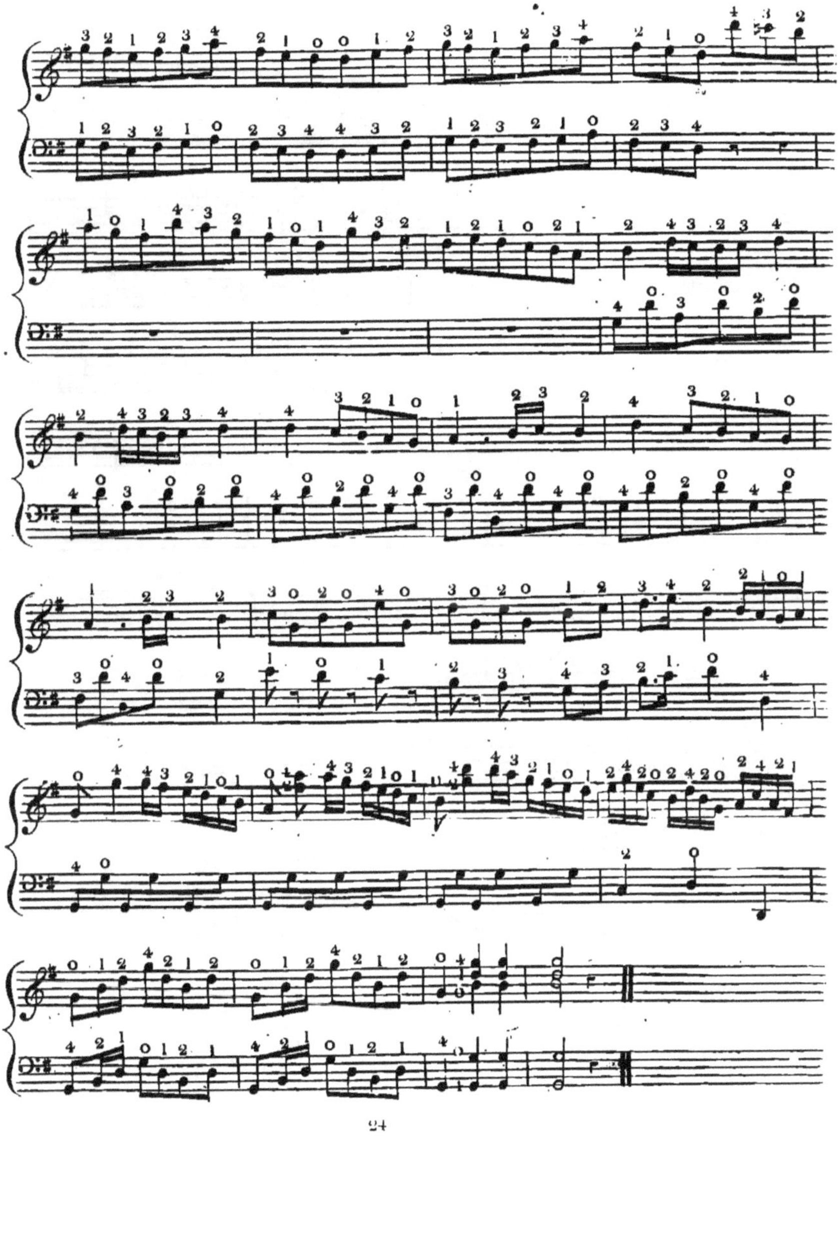

LESSON.
IV.

All⁰. Mod⁰.

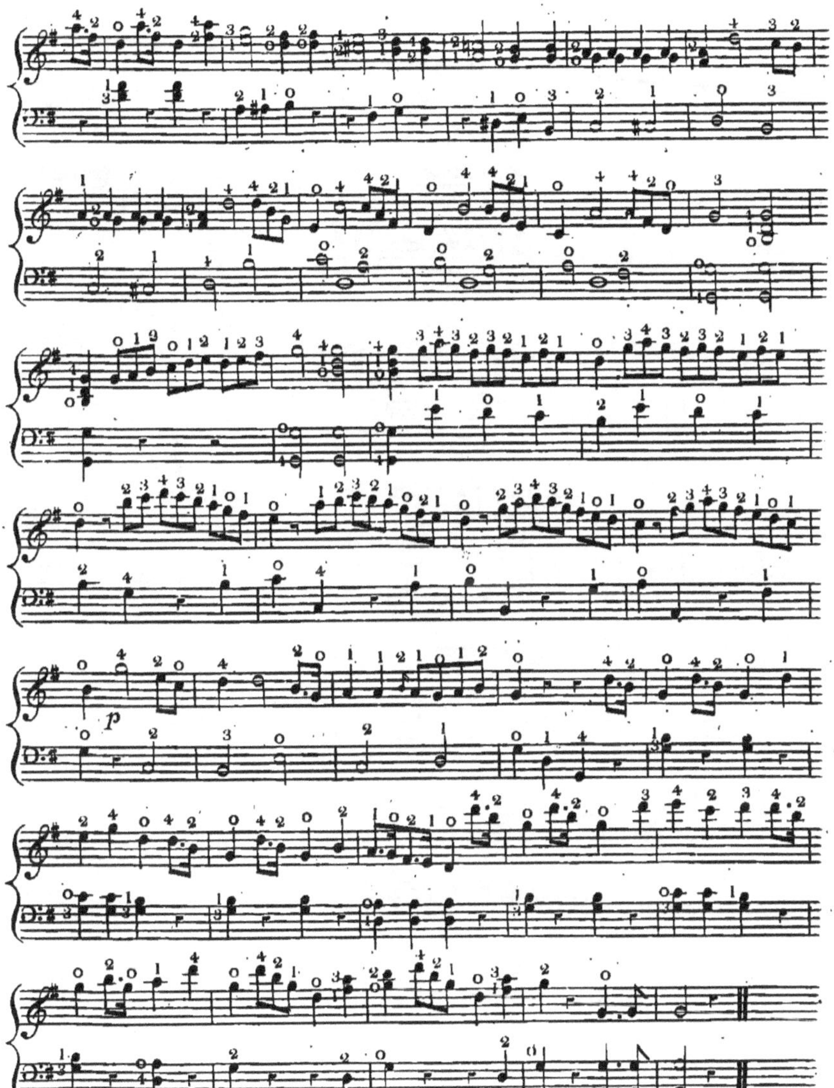

Andante

24

Andante

LESSON
V.

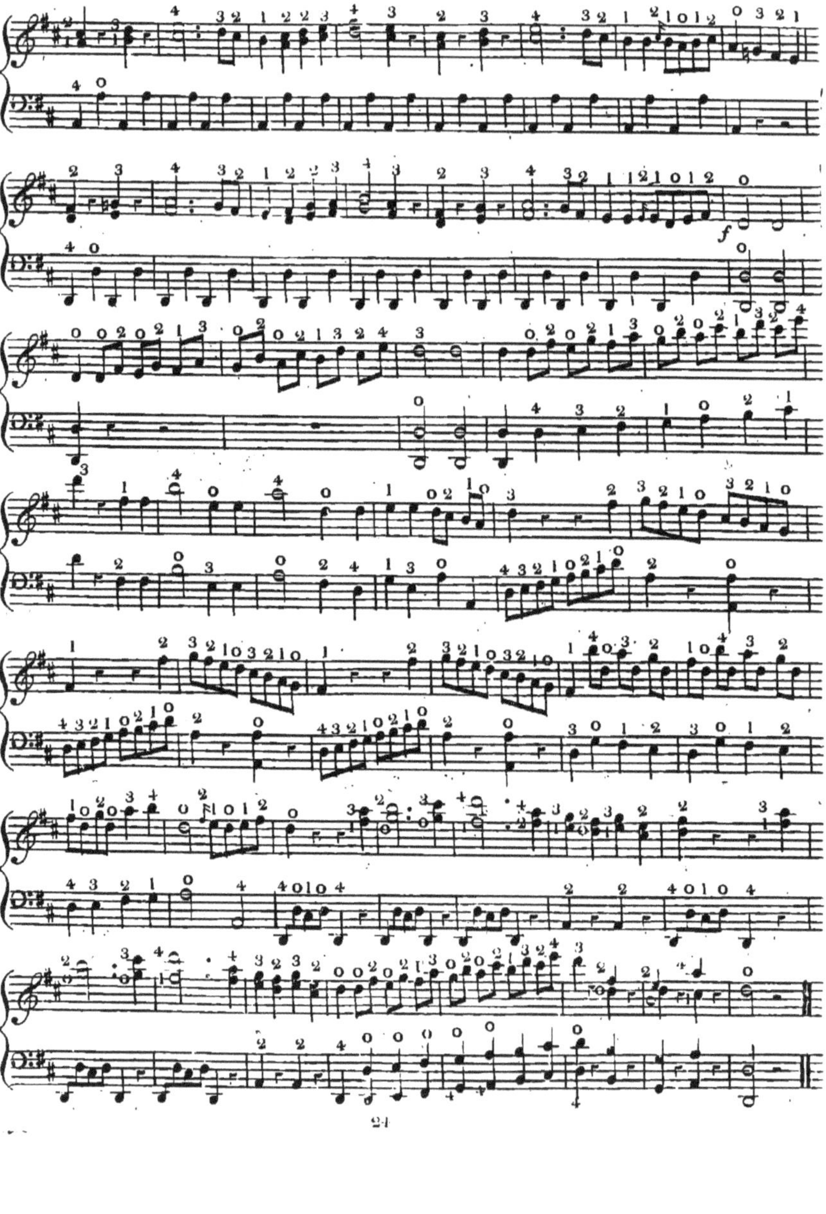

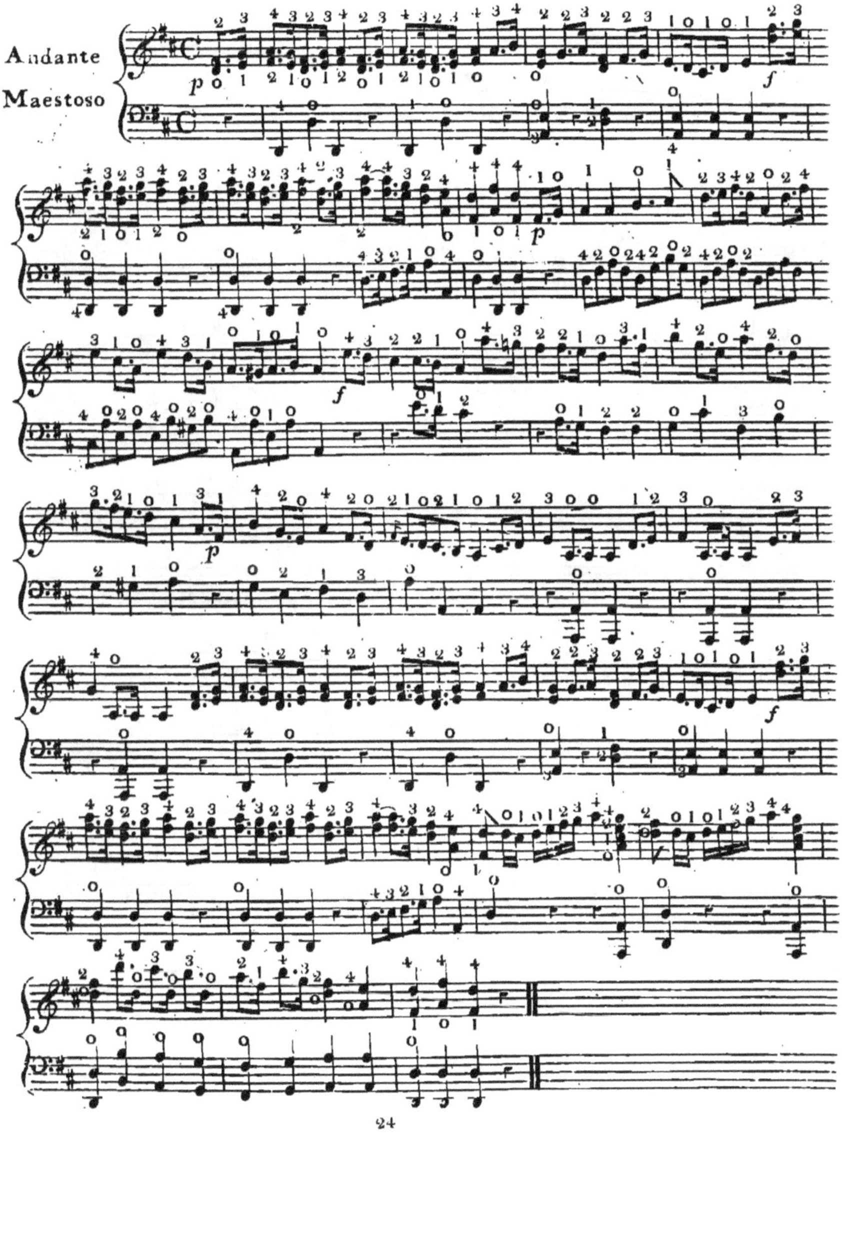
Andante
Maestoso

Allegretto

LESSON VI.

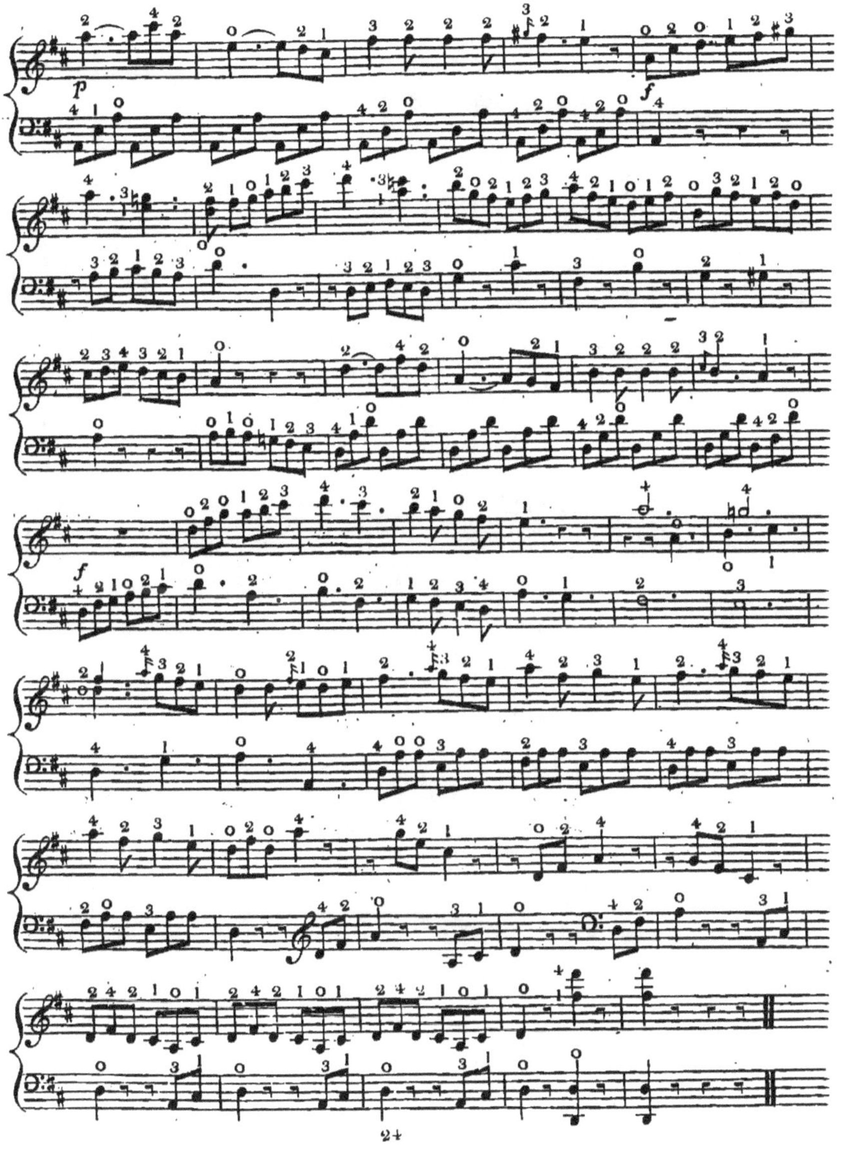
p
f
f

Larghetto

Lesson.VII
Andante.

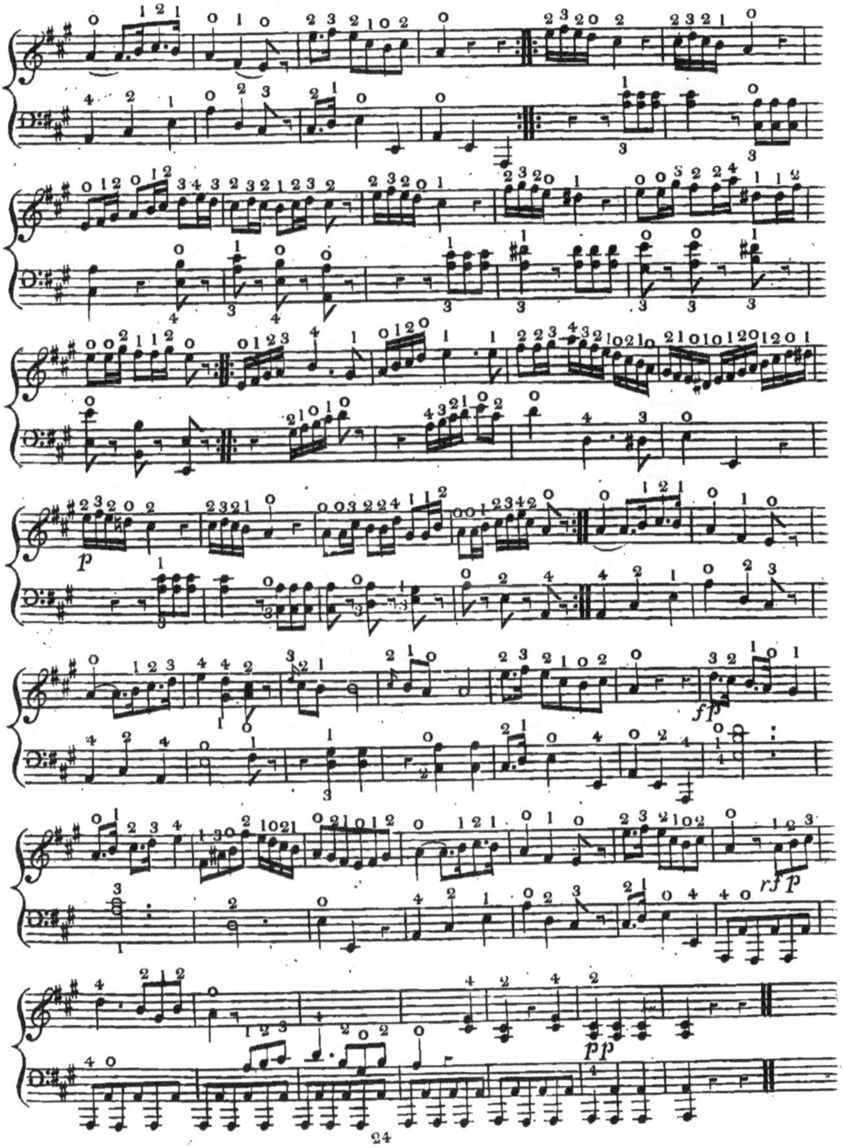
p
fp
rf p
pp

24

Brilliante

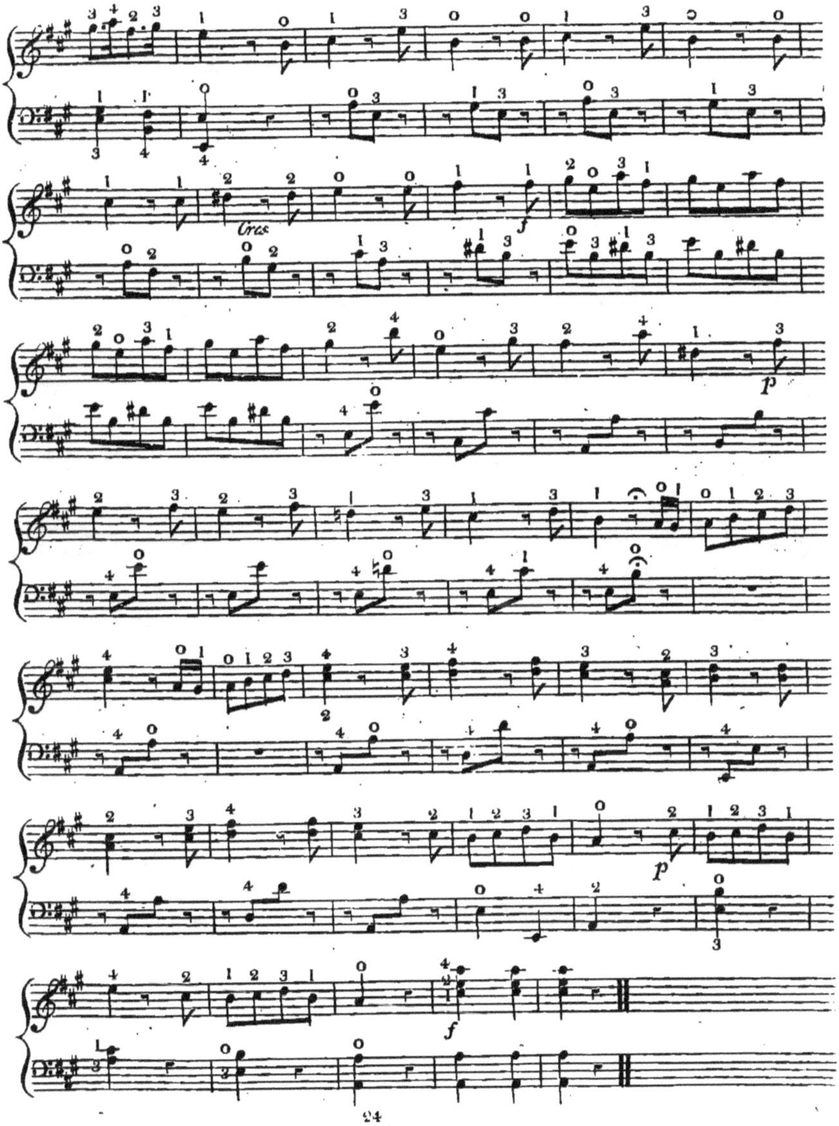
Cres

LESSON VIII

Con Spirito

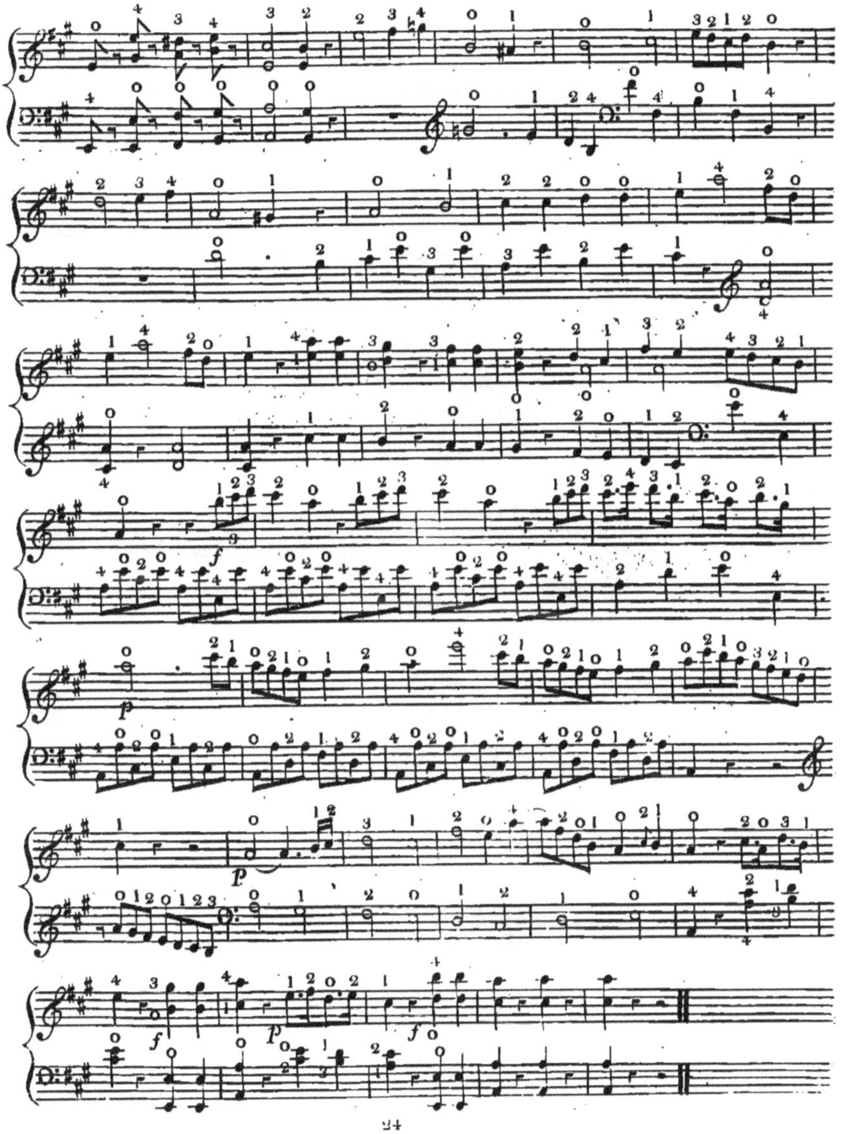

Scherzando

Fine

D.C

Major Chords

Minor Chords

To point out the Different Degrees of Movements
The following Terms are made use of.

I Degree

Moderato	Moderate
Allegretto	Rather fast
Allegro Maestoso	(Majeftic or with Elovation)
un poco Vivace	a little lively
Allegro ma non tanto Presto	lively but not too quick
Allegro un poco	a little Quick

II Degree

Allegro	Brifk
Allegro Afsai	Quicker than Allegro
Vivace, Scherzando or Brillante	Lively or merrily
poco Presto	a little Fast
Allegro con Spirito	with Spirit
Allegro con Brio	with Sprightlinefs

III Degree

Presto	Fast
Prestifsimo	very Fast
Allegro di Molto	very brifk

IV Degree

Andante ⎫ Andantino ⎬ Larghetto ⎭	Slowly

V Degree

Cantabile	In a Singing Style
Grazioso	Graceful

VI Degree

Adagio ⎫ poco Lento ⎬	Slow and Expreffive

VII Degree

Largo ⎫ Lento ⎬	very Slow

VIII Degree

Adagio Afsai ⎫ Adagio di Molto ⎬ Largo Afsai ⎭	very Slow and Solemn

Allegro

NATINA

I

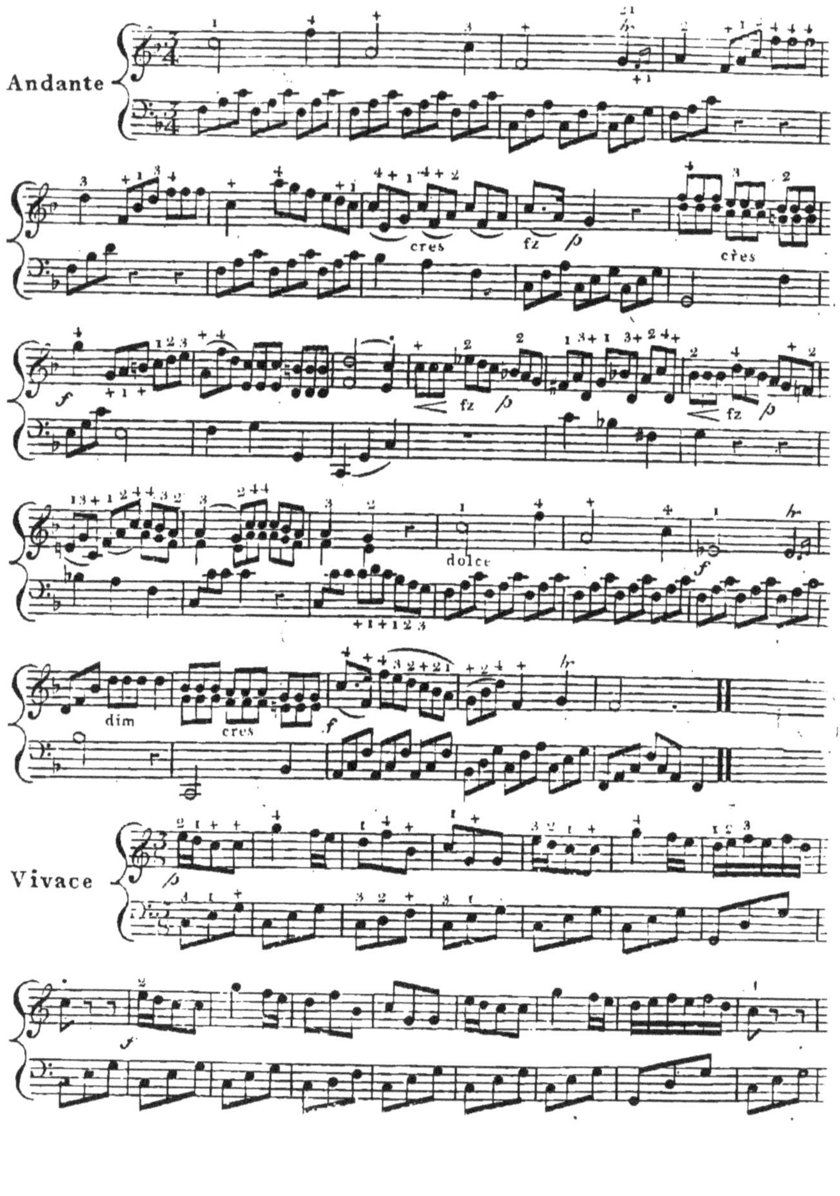
Andante
cres
fz
cres
dolce
dim
cres
Vivace

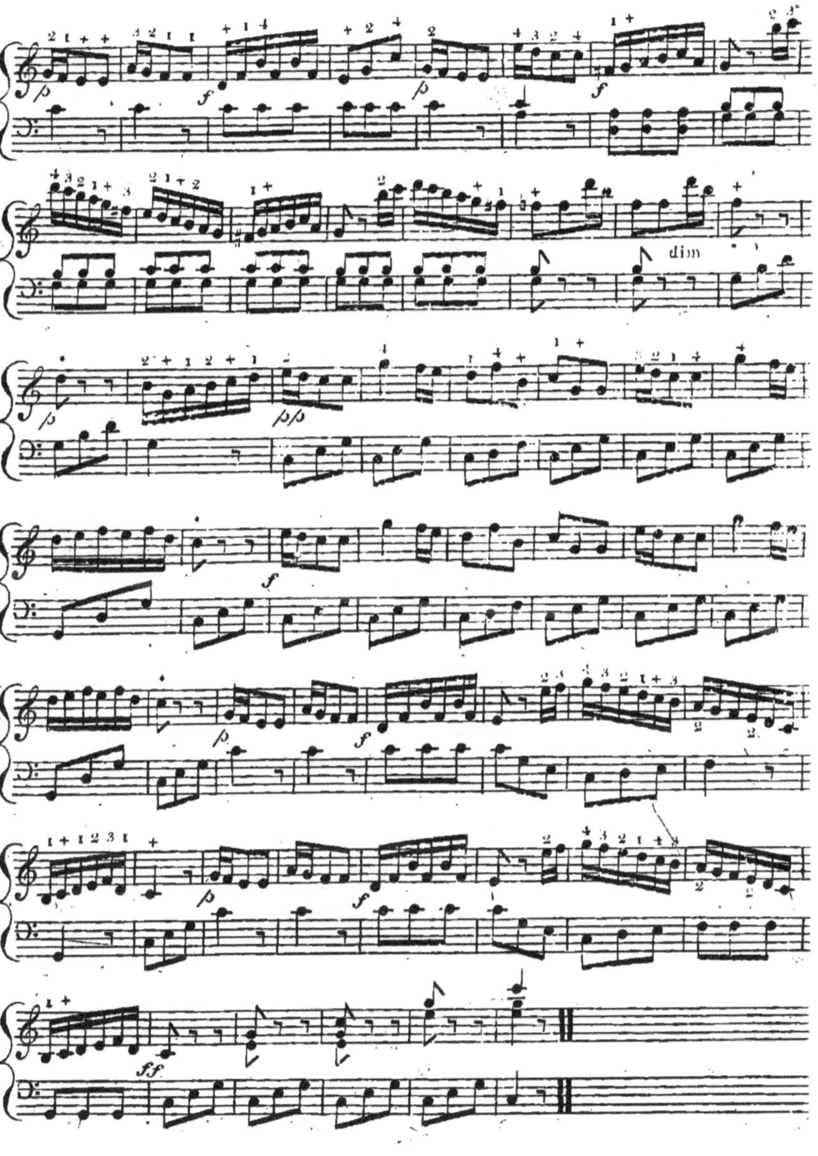
dim

SONATINA II

Allegretto

Allegretto

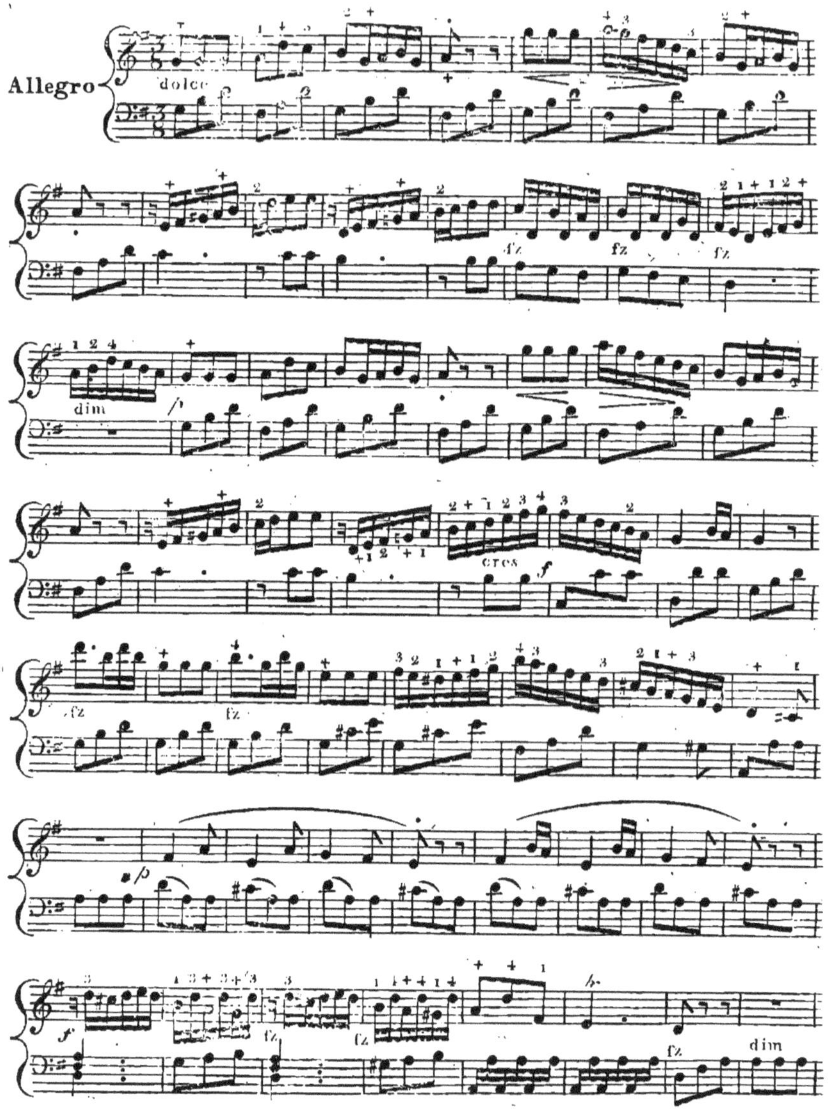
Allegro
dolce
fz
dim
p
cres
f
dim

SONATINA III

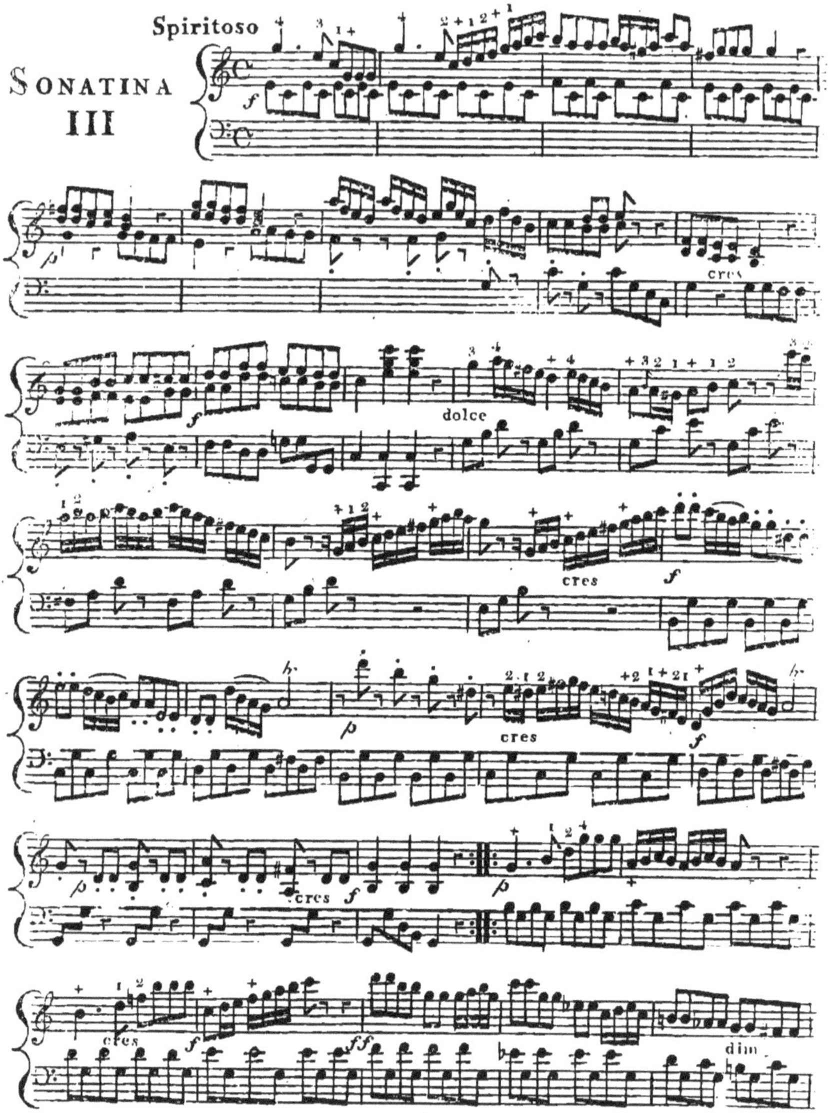

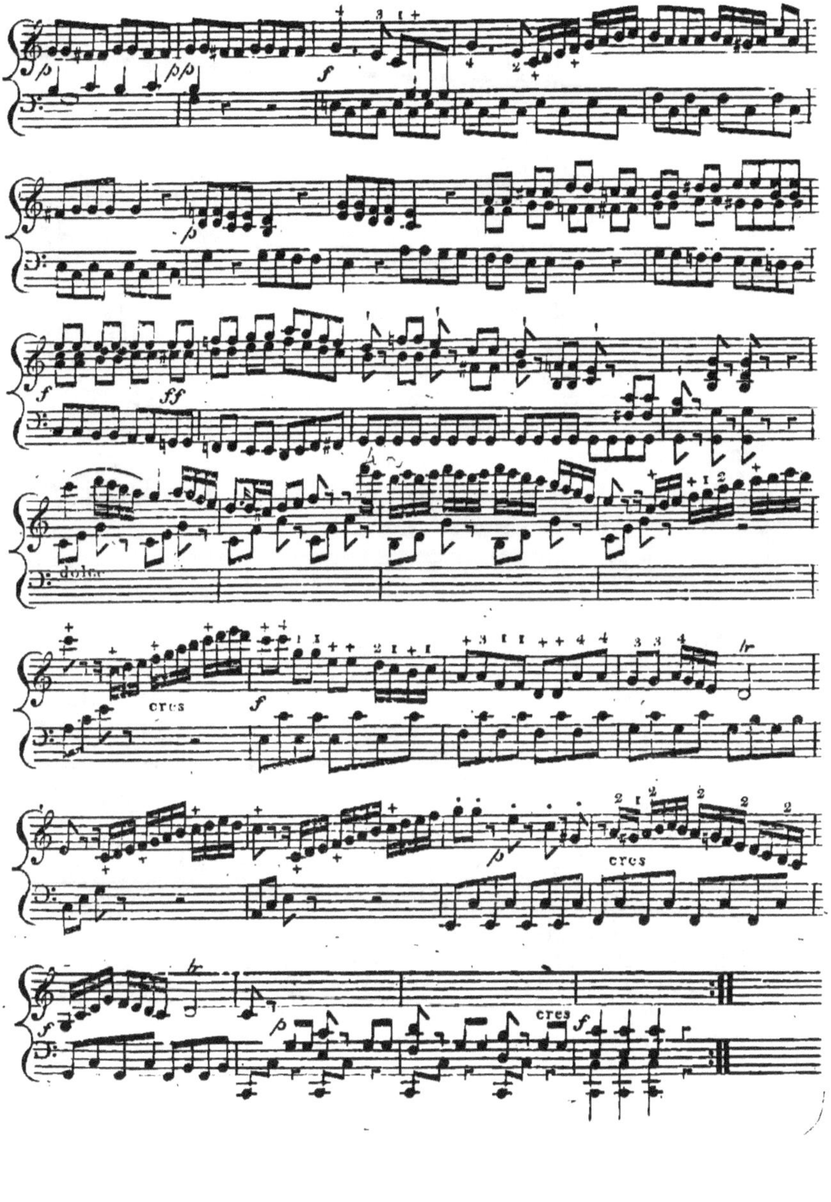
p
pp
f
ff
cres
cres
f
p
cres
f

un poco
Adagio
dolce
fz
cres
f
dim
p
dolce
cres
dim
p
Allegro
fz
p
fz
p
fz
p
fz
p
f
p
cres

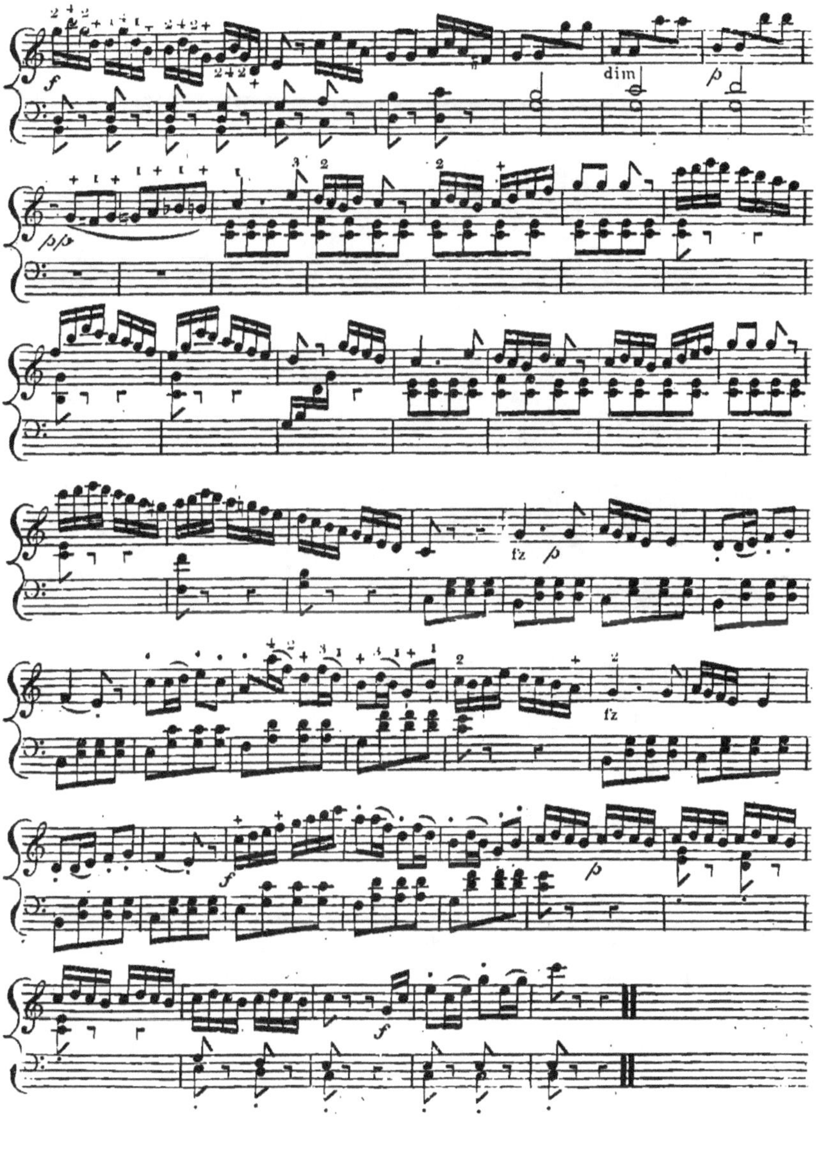
f
dim
p
pp
fz
p
fz
f
p
f

SONATINA IV

con Spirito

SONATINA
V.

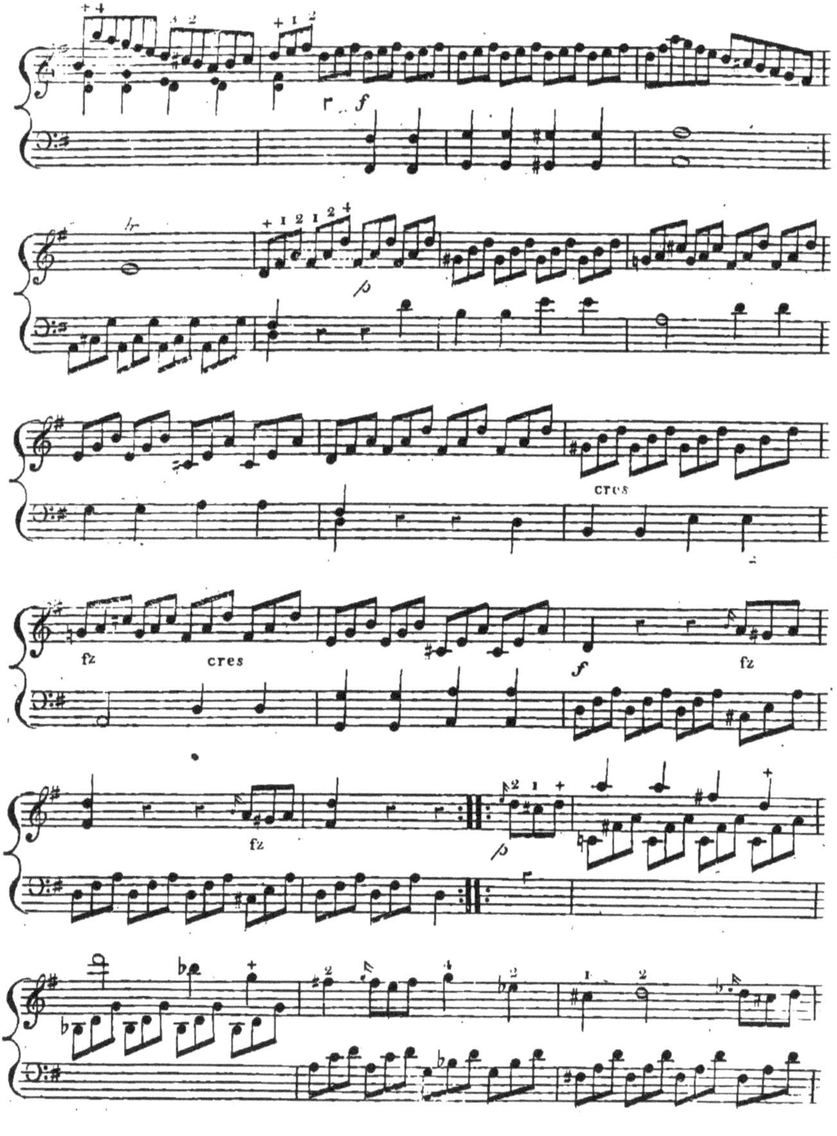
f
p
cres
fz
cres
f
fz
fz
p

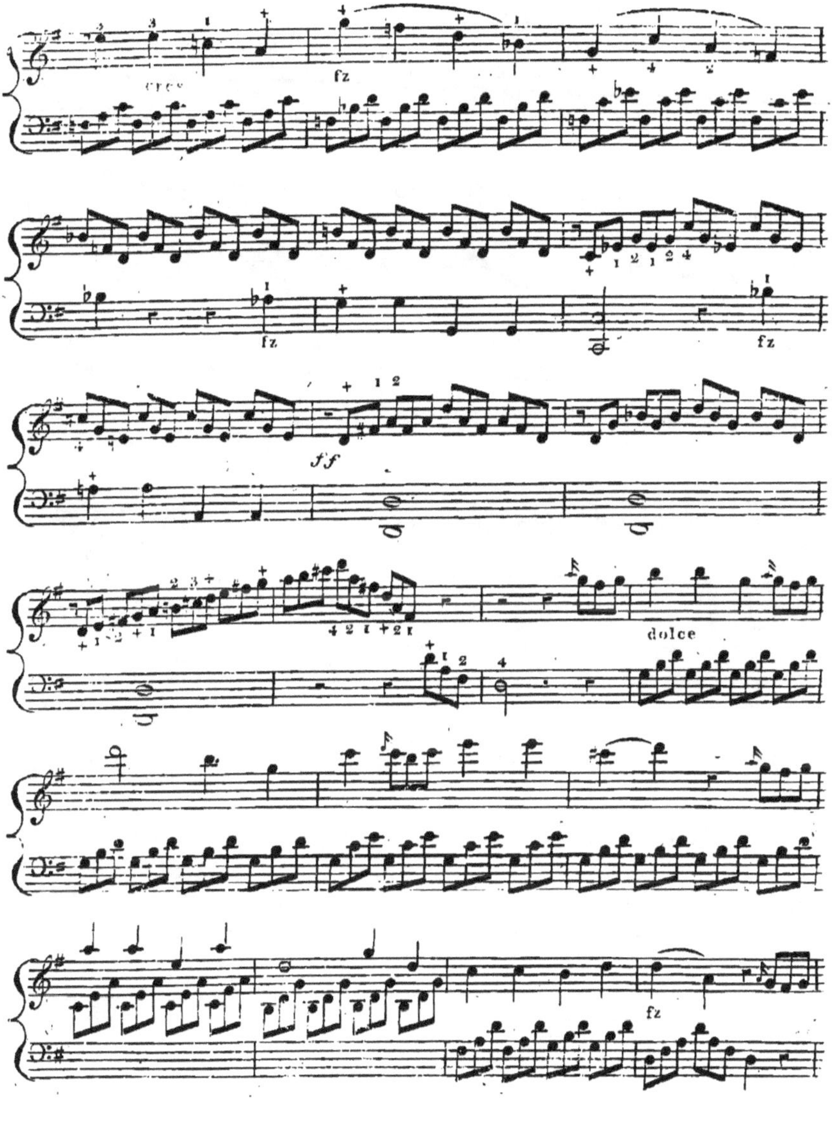
cres
fz
fz
fz
ff
dolce
fz

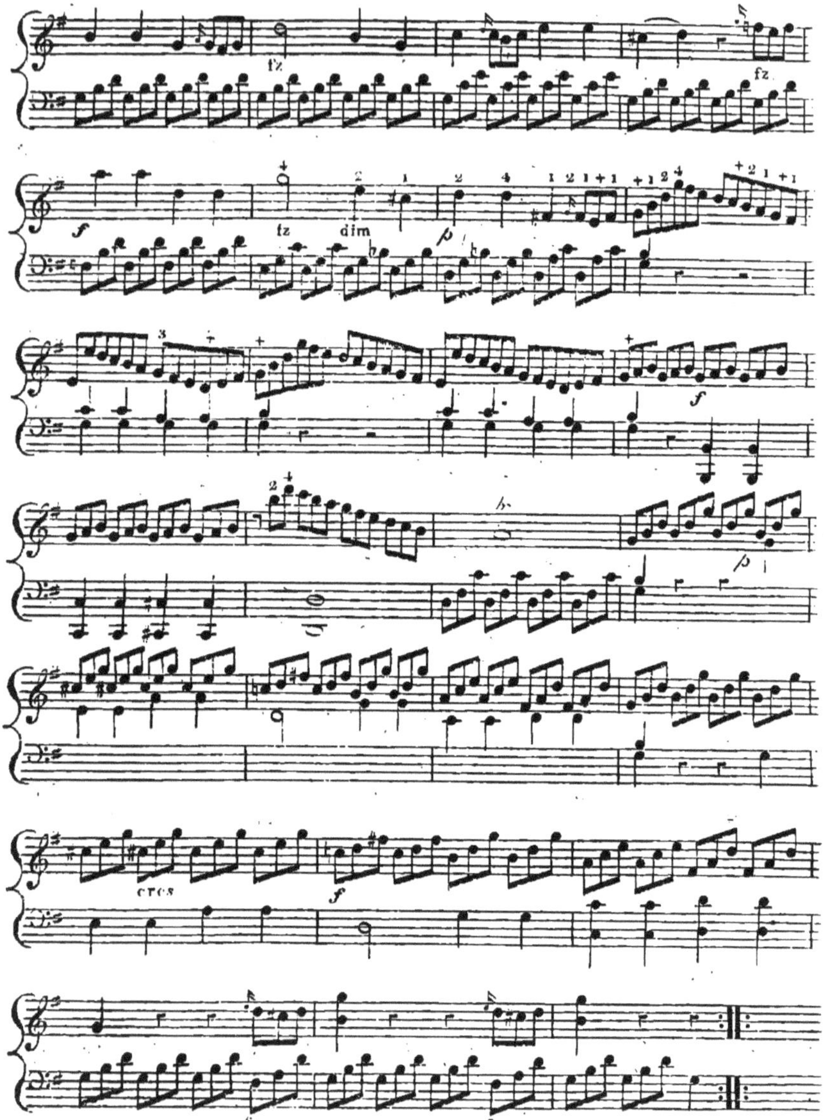
fz
fz
f
fz
dim
p
f
p
cres
f
fz
fz

ORIGINAL SWISS AIR.

Allegretto
Moderato
dolce
cres
f
p
rallentando

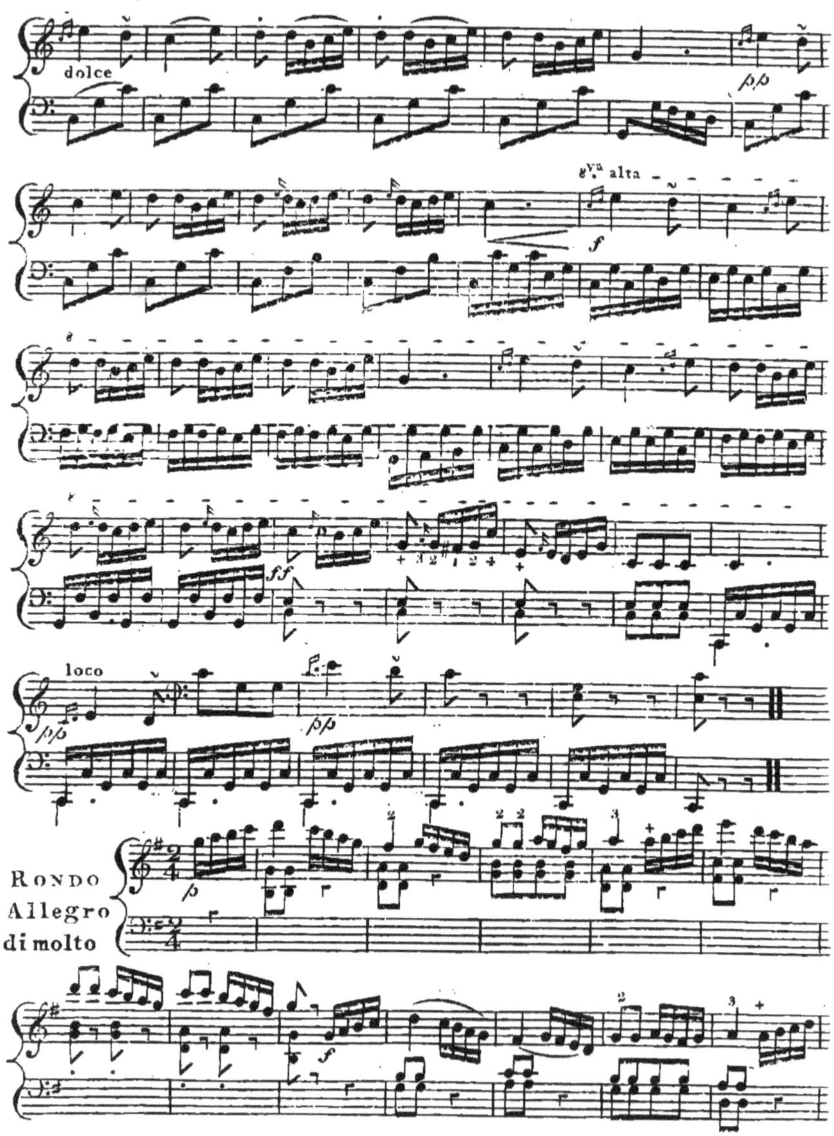
dolce
pp
8va alta
f
ff
loco
pp
Rondo
Allegro
di molto
p
f

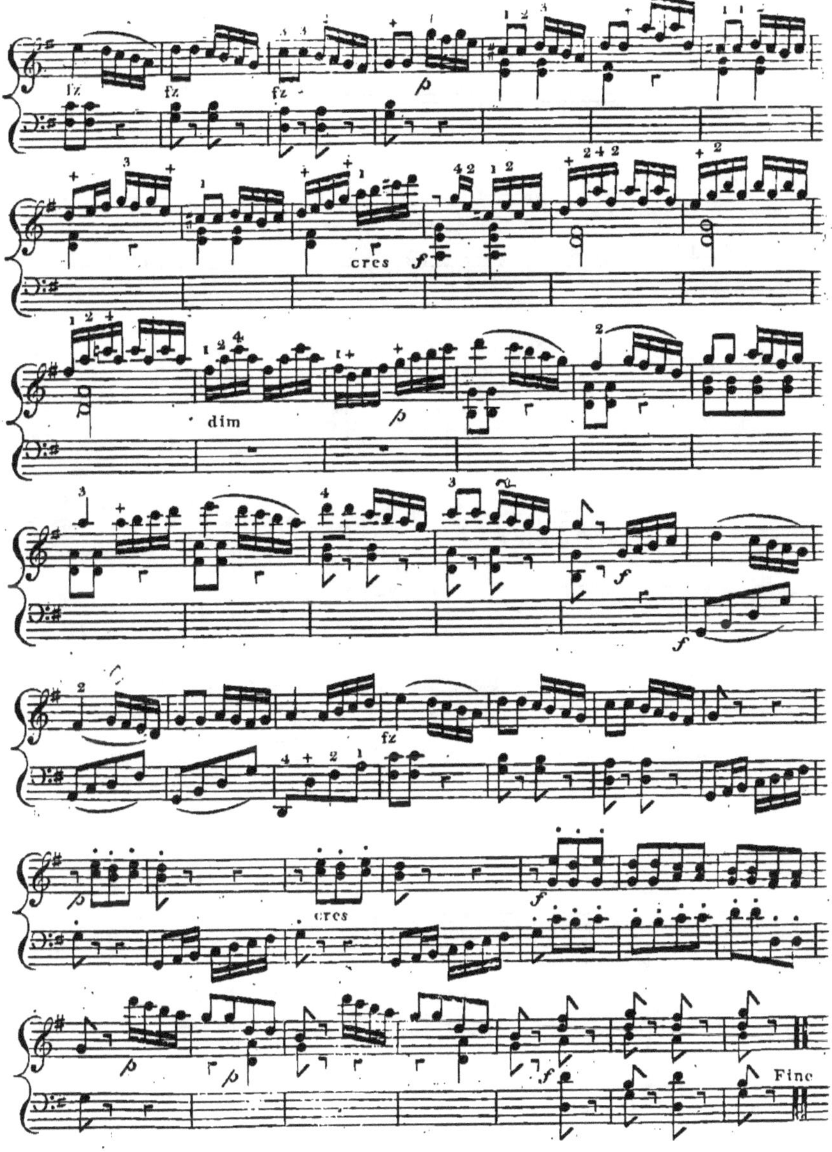
fz
fz
fz
p
cres
f
dim
p
f
f
fz
p
cres
f
p
p
f
Fine

Da Capo

Allegro con Spirito

SONATINA
VI

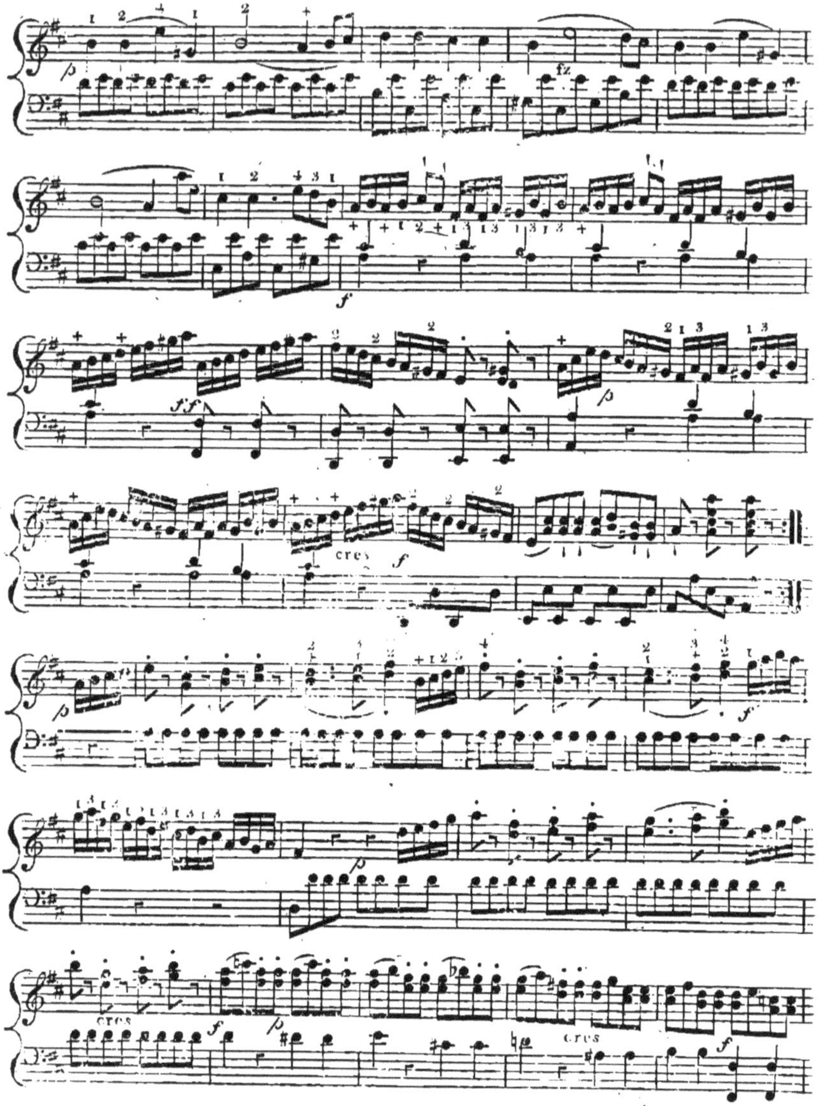
fz
cres
cres
cres

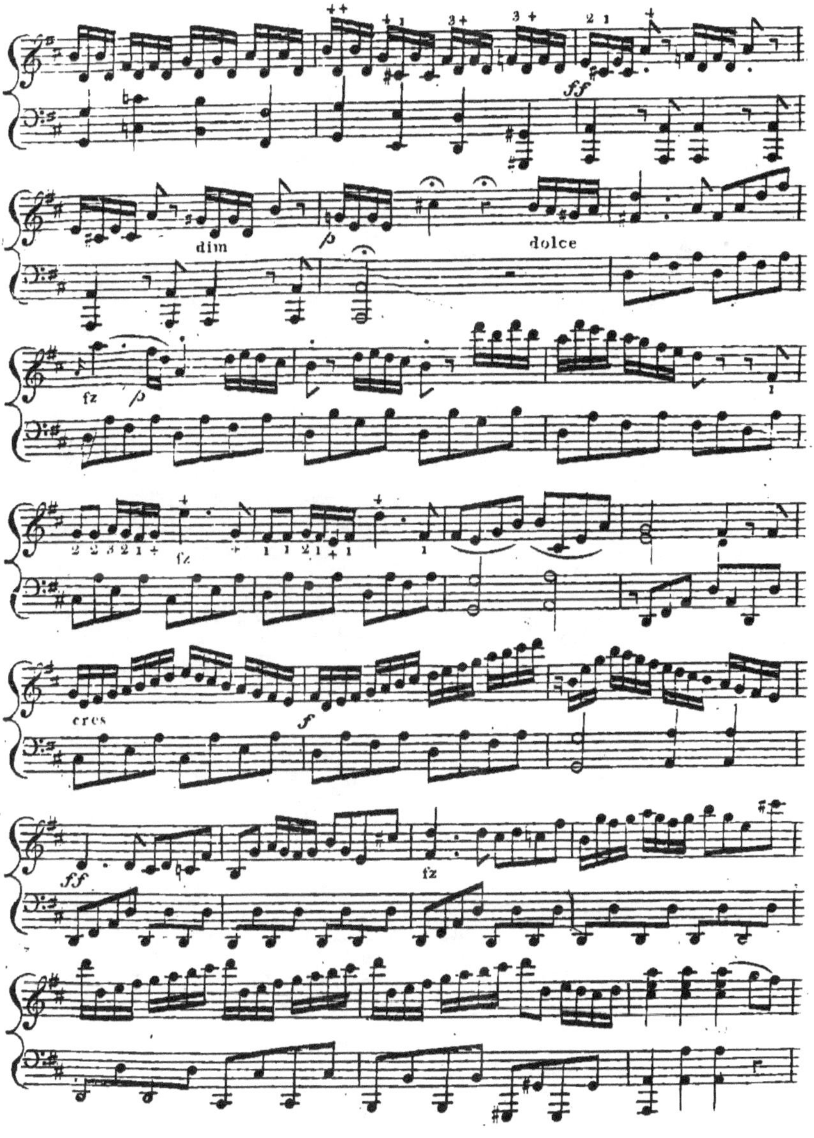
dim
dolce
cres

RONDO

Allegretto
Spiritoso

www.ingramcontent.com/pod-product-compliance
Lightning Source LLC
Chambersburg PA
CBHW021640270326
41931CB00008B/1096